Anonymous

The Opening of the Adirondacks

Anonymous

The Opening of the Adirondacks

ISBN/EAN: 9783337191078

Printed in Europe, USA, Canada, Australia, Japan

Cover: Foto ©Andreas Hilbeck / pixelio.de

More available books at **www.hansebooks.com**

Presented to the

UNIVERSITY OF TORONTO
LIBRARY

by the

ONTARIO LEGISLATIVE
LIBRARY

1980

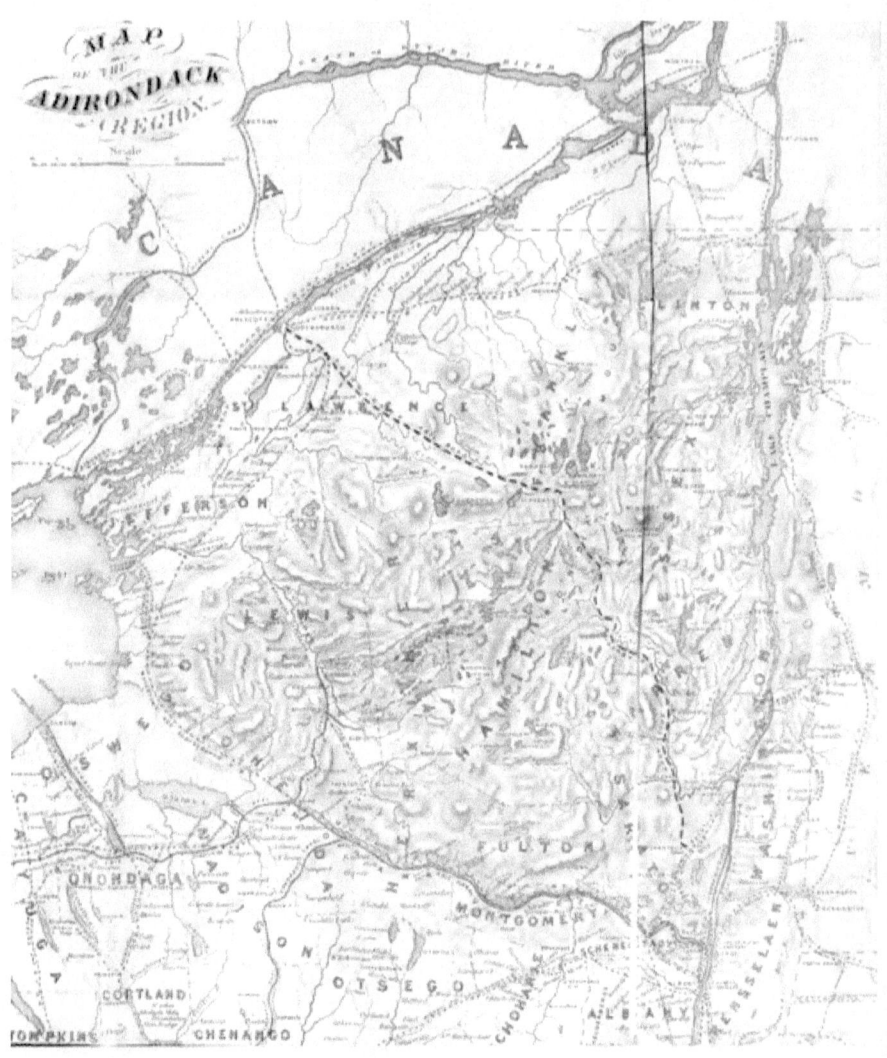

THE OPENING

OF THE

ADIRONDACKS.

WITH A MAP AND ILLUSTRATIONS.

NEW YORK:
PUBLISHED BY HURD AND HOUGHTON,
401 BROADWAY, COR. WALKER ST.
1865.

RIVERSIDE, CAMBRIDGE:
STEREOTYPED AND PRINTED BY
H. O. HOUGHTON AND COMPANY.

PREFACE.

The tract of country to which this little volume is devoted is not so well known as it should be, being generally regarded as a mere camping-ground for hunters and sportsmen, and an occasional artist in search of the wild and the picturesque, when, in fact, it possesses great capacities for mercantile and manufacturing enterprise, as well as vast mineral and forest wealth. To give some idea, however imperfect, of what it really is, and to indicate, however briefly, what it is destined to become, is the object of the present writer, who has spared neither time nor labor to insure his volume the accuracy which he believes it to possess. Among the works consulted by him while it was in progress, may be mentioned Mr. S. H. Hammond's "Hills, Lakes, and Forest Streams"; Mr. Alfred B. Street's "Woods and Waters, or the Saranac and Racket"; Mr. J. T. Headley's "The Adirondack, or Life in the Woods"; a series of papers in "Harpers' Magazine" for July, August, and September, 1859, by Messrs.

T. B. Thorpe and T. A. Richards; a series of letters written by Mr. H. J. Raymond, and published in the " New York Times " in June and July 1855; a series of letters to " The Presbyterian " of Philadelphia; and a number of articles in various other journals and magazines. " The Natural History of New York " has also been consulted, as well as Hough's " History of St. Lawrence and Franklin Counties," Redfield's " Sources of the Hudson," besides various papers in the Historical Society. Acknowledgments are likewise due Messrs. Durant, Richards, King, and others, for valuable information.

CONTENTS.

CHAPTER I.
History, Legends, Traditions 9

CHAPTER II.
Boundaries, and Geography in Detail 14

CHAPTER III.
Landscape, and Poetry of the Region 30

CHAPTER IV.
Flora and Fauna 54

CHAPTER V.
Geology, Mineralogy, Iron, Lumber, Agricultural Resources, Commerce, Manufactures, etc. . . . 60

CHAPTER VI.
Railroads; the Opening of the Adirondack . . . 77

THE OPENING OF THE ADIRONDACKS.

CHAPTER I.

HISTORY, LEGENDS, TRADITIONS.

THE region of country known as "The Wilderness of Northern New York" is almost without a history, no special work having been written on the subject, nor much, indeed, in the shape of incidental allusion, until within the last ten or fifteen years, and that chiefly in volumes of no great interest to the general public. An imaginative historian might write largely concerning it, filling

"The dark backward and abysm of time"

with pictures of the red men by whom it was undoubtedly peopled, drawing upon his fancy and the ignorance of his readers for a world of details concerning them, — their free and natural lives, their feasts, fasts, and festivals, their skill and intrepidity in the chase, their courage and scorn of death in war, — concluding the whole with a rose-colored *tableau* of the "Happy Hunting-Ground," and the poet's couplet —

> "He thinks, admitted to that equal sky,
> His faithful dog shall bear him company."

As this little volume, however, deals with *fact* and not *fiction*, the reader will have the goodness to imagine all this for himself, together with the settling of the region, or rather those adjacent, by the white races, beginning with the French, who were soon at war with the English, — a conflict in which the red men participated, and which is known in history as The French and Indian War. It was succeeded by the war of the Colonies against the Mother-country, and occasionally the din of battle rolled hitherward, disturbing the otherwise silent and peaceful wilderness. Then came the Second War with England, and, in more recent times, the unfortunate "Patriot War." But the memory of these conflicts has almost passed away, and the region is now as peaceful as it is destined to be prosperous.

It is not without its legends, — one of which we will relate, since it concerns the Indians, whom we have treated rather cavalierly perhaps. It is connected with the bell of a village-church which stands near the St. Lawrence River, and is called "The Legend of the Bell of Saut St. Louis."

A tribe of Indians having been, through the efforts of Father Nicholas, a French priest, converted to the Catholic faith, it was determined to erect a church. The sacred edifice was accordingly built; but now arose a new want: the church must have a bell. But bells in those early days were costly, and had to be procured in the Old World. A council of Indians was held, Father Nicholas presiding, and it was agreed that a certain amount of deer-skins should be contributed regularly, the value thereof being appropriated to a fund for the purchase of a bell. In due time the pious Indians, ardent in their new faith, had contributed sufficiently, and a bell was ordered from France, whence it was forwarded by the good ship "Le Grand Monarque," which was bound for the New World and Quebec.

Now it so happened that at this time a war arose between the French and English, and in consequence "Le Grand Monarque" never reached its destination, but was captured by a New-England privateer, taken into the port of Salem, there condemned as a lawful prize, and sold for the benefit of her captors. The bell was purchased by the village of Deerfield, on the Connecticut River, for a church about to be erected by the congregation of the Rev. John Williams.

This was sad news for the Indian parish of Father Nicholas. There was weeping and lamentation among the tribe. The bell, the holy bell, *their* bell, was in the hands of enemies, and not only enemies, but heretics! Heaven had afflicted them; their Great Father had visited them with sorrow; there was fasting and prayer. And there were more than these: there was a determination to recover the Sacred Bell at all hazards.

An expedition was planned against the town of Deerfield. The French under M. de Rouville, and the Indians under Father Nicholas, advanced to the town in midwinter, surprised the garrison by an ingenious stratagem, and regained their bell.

Words cannot paint the rejoicings which filled the simple hearts of the pious Indians at the fortunate capture. A general thanksgiving was proclaimed, and in a few weeks, amid the prayers and blessings of the assembled tribes, the Bell of Saut St. Louis was elevated into the belfry which had waited for it so long.

And ever since, the legend concludes, at the accustomed hour, it has sent its clear tones over the broad bosom of the St. Lawrence, to announce the hour of prayer and the lapse of time. And although its tones are shrill and feeble beside its modern companion, they possess a music, and call up an association, which will long give an interest to the Church of the Saut St. Louis, at the Indian village of Caughnawaga.

Besides this legend, and others of a more poetical cast, chiefly referring to the Indians, and evidently the invention of certain imaginative sportsmen, with whom, of late years, the Adirondacks has been a favorite hunting-ground, the region abounds in traditions mostly of "mighty hunters" and their adventures with the wild beasts of the wilderness. Around one of these personages, — a mysterious Englishman named Folingsby, who gave his name to several ponds and lakes among the Adirondacks, — a sort of poetic halo has gathered, probably because so little was known of him in his lifetime. He dwelt in a rude log-cabin, in one of the most solitary spots in the whole wilderness, supporting himself by fishing and hunting. Comrades he had none, and desired none. If a stranger, as was sometimes the case, chanced to come across his hut, he was civil, even hospitable, but never social. And he was as haughty as lonely, — a shy, reserved, mysterious man, who piqued yet baffled curiosity. There were strange rumors regarding his early history, but their truth or falsity was never known, for one wild and stormy night his troubled spirit passed away.

> "One step to the death-bed,
> And one to the bier,
> And one to the charnel,
> And one — oh where?"

He died, as he had lived, — alone.

From papers which were found in his hut after his death, it was conjectured that he was of noble birth, and had met with some terrible misfortune in his earlier years; — the lady of his love may have been false to him, or the wife of his bosom may have fled with his friend. He was buried in a rude grave, the location of which is no longer known. His memory, however, still survives in the wilderness, and is a subject for conversation around the camp-fires of a summer's night. "A haunted place," says a recent writer, "is Folingsby's Pond; and many the daring hunter or trapper, who, laughing at every other peril, trembles as night environs him in its dreaded precincts."

CHAPTER II.

BOUNDARIES, AND GEOGRAPHY IN DETAIL.

The geography of the Wilderness of Northern New York is not so definite as could be wished; most writers who have attempted to describe it differing from each other, while the majority of maps in which it is laid down are vague and unsatisfactory as regards details. Still, a general idea of it may be obtained sufficiently clear for all practical purposes.

The Wilderness of Northern New York comprises nine counties. The county of Warren lies at its southeastern corner; and on the southern line, stretching westward, extends the counties of Hamilton, Herkimer, and Lewis. On the west lies the county of Jefferson. The northern boundary is formed by the counties of Lawrence, Franklin, and Clinton, while the eastern line is the county of Essex. The region runs, in short, from Lake Champlain and Lake George on the east, to Lake Ontario and the St. Lawrence River on the west and northwest, while its northern boundary is formed by Lower Canada, and its southern by the counties of Oswego, Oneida, Fulton, and Saratoga.

BOUNDARIES AND GEOGRAPHY. 15

A great part of the region is traversed by ranges of hills and mountains, some of the latter being the loftiest in the State. In the interior are found vast, and, in many cases, unexplored forests, where deer and other species of wild animals abound. The surface is dotted with numerous lakes, which are among the most beautiful in America. Its mineral wealth is rich, though almost wholly undeveloped, while its agricultural resources are much greater than the majority of those interested in the subject have any idea of. The border lines are comparatively settled, but the interior is in every respect a wilderness.

"The Wilderness of Northern New York," says a recent tourist, "is a plateau ranging from fifteen to eighteen hundred feet above tide; it is one hundred miles in diameter. On the north and east it approaches within thirty or forty miles of the Canada line and Lake Champlain; on the south within fifteen or twenty miles of the Mohawk River, on the west within the same distance of Black River. It embraces nearly the whole of Essex, Warren, and Hamilton counties, and the southwest portion of Clinton, the south half of Franklin, the south-eastern third of St. Lawrence, the eastern third of Lewis, and the northern half of Herkimer.

"The plateau is crossed by a large valley shaped like the letter Y. This valley crosses the plateau in a northeasterly direction. It commences at the junction of Moose and Black rivers, runs seventy miles to a point south of Upper Saranac Lake, branching northerly to

Potsdam and north-easterly to Lake Champlain, near Plattsburgh. A peculiar line or chain of lakes and streams extends along this valley and its north-eastern branch. This chain of waters links Lake Champlain (through the Saranac and Racket lakes and streams, Long and Forked lakes, the Eight Lakes, and Moose and Black rivers), with Lake Ontario. The river St. Lawrence may also be considered as indirectly connected with this remarkable chain.

The waters of the plateau may be divided into *four* systems:—

The first system embraces the Saranac group of lakes and rivers. These are situated in Franklin County, and flow into Lake Champlain.

The second system lies south of the above, includes Racket River and Lake, Long Lake, Forked Lake, Tupper's Lake, etc. These flow into the river St. Lawrence.

The third group includes the Eight Lakes, the Reservoir Lakes, etc. The waters of this group flow into Lake Ontario, while the fourth system produces the Hudson River.

The eastern portion of the plateau is exceedingly mountainous, and embraces the celebrated Adirondack range of mountains, the most northerly and the most lofty in the State, superior in sublimity to the far-famed Catskills. This range extends north-easterly from Little Falls, on the Mohawk River, to Cape Trembleau at Lake Champlain, and presents conical summits cloven

into sharp gray peaks, peculiar to a hypersthene formation. Some of these peaks attain the elevation of one mile, — almost the limit of eternal snow. Mount Tahawus, or Marcy, Mount McIntyre, Mount St. Antony, Mount Colden, Mount Seward, Mount Whiteface and Dix's Peak, are some of the highest summits of this region."

And now, having given, as we hope, a tolerably clear idea of the general geography of the Wilderness of Northern New York, let us proceed to describe it more in detail, taking up the nine counties of which it is comprised in their geographical order, as they extend on the south, from east to west, and, on the north, from west to east, viz.: Essex, Warren, Hamilton, Herkimer, Lewis, Jefferson, St. Lawrence, Franklin, and Clinton.

Essex County, which stretches along the coast of Lake Champlain, is wild and mountainous, possessing all the characteristic features of a wilderness. It is traversed by the Clinton or Adirondack range of mountains, and by various other ranges, known as the Layerne Mountains, the Kayaderosseras Mountains, Schroon Mountains, etc. The most notable peaks in the county are Mount Seward, Mount Marcy, Mount Whiteface, Mount Pharaoh, Bald Mountain, and Dix's Peak. Its chief rivers are the Boquet, the Ausable, and the Schroon, the last of which is one of the sources of the Hudson; it also contains more than one hundred small lakes. Its principal settlements, or towns, are Chesterfield, Port Kent on Lake Champlain, (known in most Guide-books as "a point of departure,") Crown Point, Elizabethtown, Essex,

Moriah, Newcomb, North Elba, Tay, Schroon, West Port, etc. Near Newcomb, beside Lakes Sanford and Henderson, are the well-known Adirondack Iron-works. The famous Adirondack, or Indian Pass, one of the sublimest phenomena of nature, little inferior in grandeur to Niagara Falls, lies in this county, between Mount McIntyre and Mount Wallface.

Warren County, which lies directly south of Essex, and to the west of Lake George, is diversified by mountain-ranges similar to those in Essex County. The Hudson and Schroon rivers flow through it towards the south, and it abounds in small lakes.

Hamilton County lies west of Warren and Essex counties. It is a wild region, presenting a succession of hills, lakes, and forests, and is crossed by the Schroon, Boquet, Adirondack, and Ausable ranges of mountains. Mount Emmons is one of its principal peaks. The best known of its multitude of lakes are Long Lake, Lake Pleasant, Beaver Lake, and Piseco and Indian lakes. The Moose and Sacondago rivers flow through it. Among its towns may be mentioned Arietta, Gilman, Morehouse, and Wells. Sageville, near Lake Pleasant, is the county seat. The beautiful Racket Lake, — one of the most charming sheets of water in the New World, — lies in the northern part of this county.

Herkimer County lies west of Hamilton. Certain parts of it are wild and mountainous. The Mohawk River flows through its southern portion.

Lewis County lies between Herkimer on the east, and

Jefferson on the north and west. Much of it is literally a wilderness. It is watered by a branch of the Oswegatchie River, by the Beaver, Moose, and Indian rivers, by Independence, Otter and Fisk creeks, and the head waters of the Mohawk. It contains a number of lakes. The Black River Canal is one of its principal works of internal improvement. The county seat is Martinsburgh.

Jefferson County lies to the extreme west of Northern New York, being bounded on the western border by Lake Ontario and the St. Lawrence River. Comparatively well settled and flourishing, it is traversed by the Watertown and Rome Railroad, by the Sackett's Harbor and Ellisburgh Railroad, and the Potsdam and Watertown Railroad, which connects with Ogdensburgh. The survey of the Sackett's Harbor and Saratoga Railroad terminates here. The Black and Indian rivers and various creeks are included within its limits. It has a number of lakes, and a long line of coast and bays. Sackett's Harbor, on Lake Ontario, is its principal town. Watertown has extensive railway communication.

St. Lawrence County lies along the St. Lawrence River. It is a large and flourishing region, though as yet almost wholly undeveloped. It is watered by the Indian, Oswegatchie, Iron, Racket, St. Regis and Deer rivers, and traversed by various lines of railroads. The Ogdensburgh, or Northern Railroad, — the most northerly one in the State, — runs from Ogdensburgh on the St. Lawrence River to Rouse's Point on Lake Champlain. The Potsdam and Watertown Railroad is another important line. Steamboats connect Ogdensburgh with Montreal. It contains a number of lakes, the chief of which are Black Lake, Long Lake, and Cranberry Lake, the latter being the reservoir of the Oswegatchie River. The principal towns are Potsdam, on Racket River, Rossie, Pierrepoint, Oswegatchie, Brasher, Ogdensburgh and Russell. Canton is the county seat.

Franklin County lies between St. Lawrence and Clinton counties, its northern boundary being formed by the Canada line. Parts of it are settled, while others are wholly uncultivated. The Ausable Mountains are located here. It is watered by the Chateaugay, Salmon, Deer, St. Regis, and Racket rivers, and abounds in lakes, the most noted of which, the beautiful Saranac Lakes, lie along the southern border. The northern portion of the county is traversed by the Ogdensburgh Railroad. The principal towns are Westville, Moira, Harrietstown, Franklin, Covington, Duane, Chateaugay, Brandon, and Burke. Malone, on the Ogdensburgh Railroad, is the county seat.

Clinton County lies in the extreme north-eastern corner of the State, between Canada and Essex County and Franklin County and Lake Champlain. It contains the Ausable and other mountain ranges; the Sable, Chazy, Salmon and Saranac rivers, (most of which flow into Lake Champlain,) the Chateaugay and Chazy lakes; and is traversed by the Ogdensburgh, and Plattsburgh and Montreal railroads. Its chief towns are Altona,

Keeseville, Birmingham Falls, Beekmantown, Champlain, Chazy, Clinton, and Dannemora. Plattsburgh, on Lake Champlain, is the county seat. Rouse's Point is of importance in a military point of view. Ausable Forks, twelve miles above Keeseville, a small but flourishing town, is noted for the manufacture of nails. Altogether the county is one of the richest in the State. Its wealth in iron is immense, though its resources are far from being developed to their fullest extent.

The first settlement in St. Lawrence County was made by François Riquet, a French Sulpitian, who established an Indian mission at the mouth of the Oswegatchie, in 1749, and called it "La Presentation." In 1759 an island below the present site of Ogdensburgh was taken by the French, strongly fortified, and for a long while it successfully resisted the English. The fort erected by them also figures in the Revolutionary War. The first settlement by State authority was made by an agent of Samuel Ogden, named Ford, in 1796. After the war of 1812 the country about was settled by Yankees, and a tide of speculative emigration set towards it, but soon ebbed again. In 1837–40 came the Patriot War, and near Ogdensburgh, in November 1838, was fought the battle of Windmill Point, in which the English were victorious.

The first settlement in Franklin County was made at St. Regis, by a colony of Christianized Indians, led by Jesuit priests. This tribe still exists, half registered as American and half as English. They stand by the Catholic faith, and appear to be on the increase.

Lake Champlain and Lake George, lying on the eastern border of the counties of Clinton, Essex, and Warren, have a history of their own, with which few Americans, — certainly none who are familiar with the history of their native land, — are unacquainted.

A large portion of Franklin, St. Lawrence, Jefferson, Herkimer, and other counties, is included in what is called the "McComb Purchase," one of the largest land-purchases ever made, patented to McCormick and McComb in 1791 – 98, comprising 3,693,755 acres. This region also embraces a number of "State Lands."

Such, in brief, are the outlines of the general geography of the Wilderness of Northern New York, which embraces nearly the whole of Essex, Warren, and Hamilton, and portions of the six remaining counties. Some include the county of Fulton within its limits; others do not include the county of Jefferson. "Different portions of the Wilderness," says one authority, "are known under different names. The northern portion is called the Chateaugay Woods; the St. Regis Woods lie next below; then comes the Saranac region; then that of Racket Lake; to the east extend the Adirondacks; and below, south and south-easterly, are the Lake Pleasant region and John Brown's tract." These divisions glide into each other to a certain extent; still, this classification may be taken as a basis for a more detailed description, which we proceed to give, arranging it under four different heads or sections, corresponding to the chief divisions of the Wilderness; namely, the Northern section, or the Chateaugay and St. Regis Woods; the Middle, or the Saranac and Racket section; the Eastern, or the Adirondack section; — and the Western section, embracing St. Lawrence and Jefferson counties, and the tract containing the counties of Herkimer and Lewis. Landscapes of every variety meet and mingle in the panorama of the region, — woods, lakes, mountains, fertile plains and valleys, and barren deserts. A great confusion exists among its names: many lakes and mountains have two or more, — in fact the lakes are so numerous in some localities that they are only known by numbers.

The Northern Section of the Wilderness includes the Chateaugay and St. Regis woods, the county of Clinton, and the northern half of Franklin County. Through the eastern portion flow the Great and Little Chazy rivers, small streams, so called from Chazy Lake, a lake of some size which lies to the westward. Beyond Chazy Lake towards the west lies Bradley's Lake, and beyond this are the Chateaugay Lakes, which give their name to the neighborhood. The Upper Chateaugay Lake lies south and east of the Lower Chateaugay, with which it is connected by water; and south and east of these lies Ragged Lake, a long and narrow sheet of water with ragged outlines of coast. Westward of Ragged Lake are Ingraham's Pond, and Owl's Head Peak. The town and island of St. Regis lie on the St. Lawrence River far to the north and west, while St. Regis Lake lies to the south. The Saranac River runs through Clinton County, from the Saranac Lakes to Lake Champlain. The Salmon River also flows through a portion of this section. Near Keeseville is a romantic gorge, and in the neighborhood of Black Brook are Mount Lynn, and a collection of small ponds, known as Sampson, Taylor, Mud Ponds, etc. A number of lakes hereabout are called Slush Ponds, others enjoy the more dignified title of Military Pond. Westward of Ragged Lake lies Meacham's Pond, and to the southward of Ragged Lake lie Round Pond, Loon Lake, another Round Pond and the Rainbow Ponds.

The Middle Section embraces the Saranac Lakes, which lie in Franklin County, and are three in number. The Lower Saranac lies to the east, and the Upper Saranac to the west, while Round Lake, or more properly the Middle Saranac, lies between them and towards the south. The Upper Saranac is the larger lake, being one of the largest in the Wilderness. The lakes in this region are from one to ten miles in length, though the measurements, it must be confessed, are for the most part as confused and inaccurate as the names. North and west of the Upper Saranac lies a tract embracing what are called the Clear Lakes, or Ponds: westward are the Wolf Ponds; and south of the Saranac Lakes flows the Racket River, — a noted stream, the scenery along whose banks is wildly beautiful. Racket River flows from Racket Lake, through Forked Lake and Long Lake, through Hamilton, Franklin, and St. Lawrence counties,

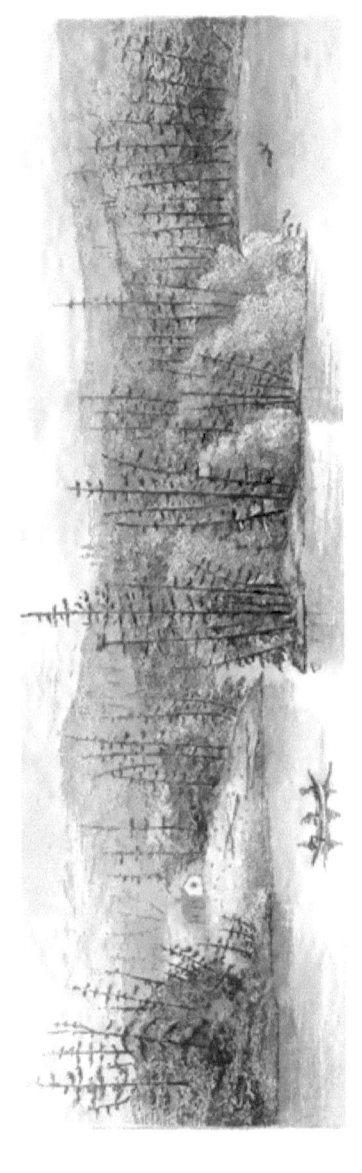

and empties itself, after a journey of one hundred and fifty miles, into the majestic St. Lawrence. "From crystal cradle to grass-green grave," says Mr. Alfred B. Street, in his picturesque *Woods and Waters*, "its shadowy footsteps glide through an unbroken wilderness. I say unbroken, for the dots of clearings only heighten by contrast the general wildness of the scene. Its name, as some suppose, is derived from the French Canadian hunters, in old times; hunting the moose in winter by means of the *raquette* (the French for snow-shoe) around the waters now known as Raquette or Racket Lake. Others affirm the name to be taken from a small marsh which a Frenchman, accompanying Indians who were exploring upward from the river's mouth, thought to be shaped like a snow-shoe. 'But I've al'ys heerd,' said Harvey, 'the name came from the tarnal racket the river keeps up with the falls, and the rafts and what not on 't.' To return, however. North of Racket Lake, which lies in the northern part of Hamilton County, are Long and Forked Lakes, so called from their peculiar shape, and east of it are the Eckford chain of lakes. Not far from Forked Lake is Brandreth Lake, which derives its name from the well-known maker of pills, who owns a considerable tract of land in the vicinity. South and west of the Saranac Lakes, and north of Forked and Long Lakes, lies Tupper's Lake, a charming sheet of water, whose beauties are the delight of the tourist. Into this lake flows Bog River, and near it rises Mount Morris. Connected with it on the north are Racket Pond and Racket River, which connect with Stony Pond and Creek and the Saranac Lakes, between which stretches the passage known as the Indian Carry. It is one of the characteristics of the waters of this region that they are all closely connected with each other, affording admirable facilities for internal and canal communication. In this neighborhood are Simon's and Folingsby's Ponds, the last of which is named after the lonely hunter of whom we have already spoken. West and north of the Saranac Lakes are Rawlin's, Floodwood, Slang, Turtle, Hoel's, and other lakes and ponds, the Fish-creek waters, etc. On the Racket River are Racket Falls, not far from Long Lake, and the Perciefield Falls; south of the Eckford Lakes are the Chain Lakes; north of the Lower Saranac Lake lies Colesby's Pond; and south of the Saranac Lakes is Mount Seward, one of the highest peaks in the region.

The Eastern, or Adirondack Section comprises the eastern part of Hamilton, and the whole of Essex County. It is a mountainous region, diversified with numerous lakes. South of Mount Seward lie the Preston Ponds and Mount Henderson; and to the east of the latter Lake Henderson, on the south of which lies a larger sheet of water known as Lake Sanford. The village of Adirondack, and the Adirondack Iron-works, lie on these lakes. West of Sanford and Henderson lakes lie Newcomb Lake, Delia Lake, Catlin Lake, the Rich Pond, Moose Lake, etc.; and north of Lake Henderson lies Lake Placid, near which are MacKenzie's Pond and Sugar-Loaf Mountain. Between these on the north and Lake

Henderson on the south, dividing Mount Wallface and Mount McIntyre, stretches the sublime Indian or Adirondack Pass; north and east of which rises Mount Whiteface, one of the noblest peaks in the New World. In this mountain is a chasm or gorge, known as the Whiteface Notch; not far from which rises Mount Esther. In the northern and eastern portion of Essex County are Lake Colden, and Lake Walauche, the Jay Mountains, Poke-a-Moonshine Mount, and other mountains and lakes. South and east of Mount Whiteface rises Mount Marcy, or Tahawus — the Mount Blanc of the Wilderness; to the southward lie the Ausable Ponds, Nipple Top Mount, Dix's Peak, McComb's Mount, Boreas Lake and Mount; to the east are the Boquet Mountains and river, Bald Mount, Bartlett Mount, etc. Directly to the south of Essex County lies Paradox Lake, and Mount Pharoah and lake, and south of Paradox Lake, Lake Schroon, the source of the river of that name. In Warren County are Trumbull Mount, Black Tongue Mount, Cathead Mount, Prospect Mount, French Mount, besides a number of other mountains and lakes, which lie towards the east near Lake George. Lake Layerne lies towards the south near the Hudson River, and to the west are Crane, Whortleberry and Gore mountains; in the interior are Loon Lake, Fiend Lake, Brant Lake, and others. The region is watered by the Schroon, Boreas and Boquet rivers, and various other streams.

The Western Section comprises St. Lawrence County principally, and the larger portion of Jefferson, Herkimer and Lewis counties. It is watered towards the north by the St. Regis, Racket, and Grass rivers, and towards the west and south by the Oswegatchie River. Black Lake, which is of considerable size, lies towards the west; along the southern boundary are Yellow, Silver, Pleasant and Clear lakes; and towards the east are Geanekee Lake, Marawepie Lake, Ambee Lake, and Jordan and Trout lakes. Jefferson County, south and east of St. Lawrence County, is watered by the Black River, the Indian and Chaumont rivers, and other streams. Towards the north lie Mud, Millstone, Grass, Butterfield, Hyde, Red, Moon, and Vroman's lakes, and in the interior are Perch River and lake. Between Jefferson County on the west, and the Racket Lake region on the east, stretch the counties of Lewis and Herkimer, and to the south of Racket Lake, in Hamilton County, lies the Lake Pleasant region. John Brown's Tract extends in this locality. The Indian Lake and Indian and Jessup rivers, are in the southern half of Herkimer County. Further south are Lewey Lake, Mason Lake, Echo Lake, Long Lake, Elm Lake, Gilman's Lake, Round Lake, Oxbow Lake, and Lake Pleasant; south of these are Piseco Lake, Spy Lake, Morehouse Lake, and the Sacondaga River; and to the west lie many small lakes and ponds. West of these, and in Herkimer County, are Transparent Lake, the Reservoir Lakes, the Eight Lakes, and a long extent of wilderness. This region is traversed by branches of the Beaver and Moose rivers, the latter of which flows in Lewis County, as does also Otter Creek, Independence Creek, and Black River, Deer and Indian rivers, and the west branch of the Oswegatchie. Lake Bonaparte and Oswegatchie Pond lie in the northern part of this district, and lower down are Beaver, Crystal, and Brantingham lakes.

CHAPTER III.

LANDSCAPE, AND POETRY OF THE REGION.

The Wilderness of Northern New York is the most unique tract of country now remaining within the limits of the United States, if not of the New World itself. It represents in its wilder localities the ancient condition of the Continent as it existed for untold centuries under the dominion of the red races by whom it was sparsely peopled, — a wild, vast, primitive territory which it is difficult for even the imagination to realize. Other portions of the land are perhaps as wild, — clad in as dense forests, watered by as lonely lakes, and crowned by as lofty mountains, — but they are limited in comparison, their ancient depths more readily yielding to the foot of the hunter and the trapper, the true pioneers of civilization, and their borders more rapidly disappearing before the axe of the woodman. Certainly there is no such wilderness east of the Rocky Mountains. One might expect to find it, or its fellow, somewhere in the far-off West, that mythical land which is every day drawing nearer to us, — but not on the Eastern side of the Continent, — not in the Northern States, and assuredly not in the great State of New York, where its existence to-day is little short of a miracle.

The geography of the region as we have indicated it in the previous chapter, may give some idea of its extent; but its varied character, the manifold forms of its scenery, are not to be described in the brief compass of a work like this. Our minds are conventionally unfitted, our imaginations too limited, or not sufficiently active, to picture its grandeur and magnificence. Conceive it if you can as it is; millions of acres, hundreds of miles of wilderness, here stretching away in the distance, there sinking into deep and broad valleys, and there swelling up the sides of hills and mountains which it clothes to the very summits. Miles of primeval woods, dense, dark, and silent, — a bewildering waste of trees, an interminable mass of trunks, which you can scarcely distinguish, so thick the boughs around, and so impervious the roof overhead; dense, save where some adventurous hunter has made a clearing; dark, save where the noonday sun contrives to pierce the thinnest shield of greenery with his sharp, bright arrows; and silent, save for the twitter of birds, the whine or roar of some wild beast, the whisper of streams and brooks, and the low, soft, sea-like, everlasting murmur of the wind in the trembling leaves. Here and there are small lakes and small streams, threads of silver winding away through the shadows; and yonder, rising and falling, are mountains which shut you in like a wall, wooded to the peaks, which are bleak and bare, or white and cloud-like with snow.

Such, in outline at least, is the Wilderness of Northern New York, and such it has been from immemorial years. Across the background of its Past, however, flits a procession of dusky figures,— dim, distant, and unreal as the shadows of a dream. How they, and the dead and gone time in which they once lived can become

> "Such sights as youthful poets dream
> On summer eves by haunted stream,"

let the most American of all our poets tell us.

> "Then all this youthful paradise around,
>   And all the broad and boundless mainland, lay
> Cooled by the interminable wood, that frowned
>   O'er mount and vale, where never summer ray
>   Glanced, till the strong tornado tore his way
> Through the gray giants of the sylvan wild;
>   Yet many a sheltered glade, with blossoms gay
> Beneath the showery sky and sunshine mild,
> Within the shaggy arms of that dark forest smiled.
>
> There stood the Indian hamlet, there the lake
>   Spread its blue sheet that flashed with many an oar,
> Where the brown otter plunged him from the brake,
>   And the deer drank: as the light gale flew o'er,
>   The twinkling maize-field rustled on the shore;
> And while that spot, so wild, and lone, and fair,
>   A look of glad and guiltless beauty wore,
> And peace was on the earth and in the air,
> The warrior lit the pile, and bound his captive there.
>
> Not unavenged, the foeman, from the wood,
>   Beheld the deed; and when the midnight shade
> Was stillest, gorged his battle-axe with blood:
>   All died — the wailing babe — the shrieking maid —

LANDSCAPE AND POETRY.

> And in the flood of fire that scathed the glade
> The roofs went down; but deep the silence grew,
>   When on the dewy woods the daybeam played;
> No more the cabin-smokes rose wreathed and blue,
> And ever, by their lake, lay moored the bark canoe."

Better than this, however, is the following glimpse of savage life, — a characteristic picture which only a fine artist could have painted. It is from Bryant's noble poem, "The Fountain."

> "I behold
> The Indian warrior, whom a hand unseen
> Has smitten with his death-wound in the woods,
> Creep slowly to thy well-known rivulet
> And slake his death-thirst. Hark, that quick, fierce cry
> That rends the utter silence: 't is the whoop
> Of battle, and a throng of savage men,
> With naked arms and faces stained with blood,
> Fill the green wilderness: the long bare arms
> Are heaved aloft, bows twang and arrows stream;
> Each makes a tree his shield, and every tree
> Sends forth its arrow. Fierce the fight and short,
> As is the whirlwind. Soon the conquerors
> And conquered vanish, and the dead remain
> Mangled by tomahawks. The mighty woods
> Are still again, the frighted bird comes back
> And plumes her wings; but thy sweet waters run
> Crimson with blood. Then, as the sun goes down,
> Amid the deepening twilight, I descry
> Figures of men that crouch and creep unheard,
> And bear away the dead. The next day's shower
> Shall wash the tokens of the fight away."

Enough, however, of that poetic myth — the Noble

Savage. Let us return to the forest as it is to-day, — lone, shadowy, and peaceful.

> " The thick roof
> Of green and stirring branches is alive
> And musical with birds, that sing and sport
> In wantonness of spirit; while below
> The squirrel, with raised paws and form erect,
> Chirps merrily. Throngs of insects in the shade
> Try their thin wings and dance in the warm beam
> That waked them into life. Even the green trees
> Partake the deep contentment; as they bend
> To the soft winds, the sun from the blue sky
> Looks in and sheds a blessing on the scene.
> Scarce less the cleft-born wild-flower seems to enjoy
> Existence than the winged plunderer
> That sucks its sweets. The mossy rocks themselves,
> And the old and ponderous trunks of prostrate trees
> That lead from knoll to knoll, a causey rude,
> Or bridge the sunken brook, and their dark roots,
> With all their earth upon them, twisting high,
> Breathe fixed tranquillity. The rivulet
> Sends forth glad sounds, and tripping o'er its bed
> Of pebbly sands, or leaping down the rocks,
> Seems, with continuous laughter, to rejoice
> In its own being. Softly tread the marge,
> Lest from her midway perch thou scare the wren
> That dips her bill in water. The cool wind,
> That stirs the stream in play, shall come to thee,
> Like one that loves thee, nor will let thee pass
> Ungreeted, and shall give its light embrace."

Such are the woods in summer.

> " But Winter has yet brighter scenes, — he boasts
> Splendors beyond what gorgeous Summer knows;

Or Autumn with his many fruits, and woods
All flushed with many hues. Come when the rains
Have glazed the snow, and clothed the trees with ice,
While the slant sun of February pours
Into the bowers a flood of light. Approach!
The incrusted surface shall upbear thy steps,
And the broad arching portals of the grove
Welcome thy entering. Look! the massy trunks
Are cased in the pure crystal; each light spray,
Nodding and tinkling in the breath of heaven,
Is studded with its trembling water-drops,
That glimmer with an amethystine light.
But round the parent stem the long low boughs
Bend, in a glittering ring, and arbors hide
The glassy floor. Oh! you might deem the spot
The spacious cavern of some virgin mine,
Deep in the womb of earth — where the gems grow,
And diamonds put forth radiant rods and bud
With amethyst and topaz, — and the place
Light up, most royally, with the pure beam
That dwells in them. Or haply the vast hall
Of fairy palace, that outlasts the night,
And fades not in the glory of the sun; —
Where crystal columns send forth slender shafts
And crossing arches; and fantastic aisles
Wind from the sight in brightness, and are lost
Among the crowded pillars. Raise thine eye;
Thou seest no cavern roof, no palace vault;
There the blue sky and the white drifting cloud
Look in. Again the wildered fancy dreams
Of spouting fountains, frozen as they rose,
And fixed, with all their branching jets, in air,
And all their sluices sealed. All, all is light;
Light without shade. But all shall pass away
With the next sun. From numberless vast trunks,
Loosened, the crashing ice shall make a sound

<pre>
          Like the far roar of rivers, and the eve
        Shall close o'er the brown wood as it was wont."
</pre>

The grandest feature of the region, however, is not the forests in which it has slept so many centuries, green with the mantle of summer, and white with winter's snows, but the ranges of mountains by which it is traversed, shooting up here and there into lofty peaks, which can be seen in clear weather at a great distance. The most noted of these is Mount Tahawus, or Marcy, which was ascended some years ago by Mr. Headley, who thus describes his ascent: —

"We strained forward, now treading over a springy marsh, now stooping and crawling like lame iguanas, through a swamp of spruce-trees, and anon following the path made by deer and moose, as they came from the mountains to the streams, or climbing around a cataract, until, at length, we reached Lake Colden, perfectly embosomed amid the gigantic mountains, and looking for all the world like an innocent child sleeping in a robber's embrace. Awfully savage and wild are the mountains that enclose this placid sheet of water. Crossing a strip of forest we next struck the Opalescent River, so called from the opals found in its bed. The forest here is almost impassable, and so for five miles we kept the bed of the stream, chasing it backward to its source. The channel is one mass of rocks; and hence our march was a constant leap from one to another, requiring a correct eye, and a steady foot, to keep the balance. Thus, zigzagging over the bed of this turbulent stream, we flitted

backward and forward, like flies over the surface of a river, till, at length, I heard a shout. S——th had missed his footing, and slipping from a rock, gone plump into a deep pool. Gathering himself up, he laughed louder than the loudest, and pushed on."

The party soon came to a halt, and cooked their dinner on the rocks. "Soon after," he continues, "our packs were all slung again, and we on the march. We continued diving deeper and deeper into the hills, until we at last reached the base of the mountain, and the foot of a lofty cataract. I have climbed the Alps and the Apennines, but never found foot and eye in such requisition before. It was literally 'right up,' while the spruce-trees, with their dry limbs like thorns a yard long, stuck out on every side, ready to transfix us, and compelling us to duck and dodge at every step. Now sinking through the treacherous moss that covered some gap in the rocks, and now swinging from one dead tree to another, we continued for two miles panting and straining up the steep acclivity, flogged and torn at every step. We had already gone fifteen miles, and such a winding up the tramp was too much. H—— thought 'the Millerites had better start from this elevation.' A—— said 't would 'tear their ascension-robes so that they would look rather shabby on the wing.' T—— was sure the notion would take with them, as they

"'Could make such a *dale* of the journey on *foot*.'

"One large, athletic hunter we had taken along as an

assistant, gave out, so that we were compelled frequently to halt, and let him rest. The fir-trees grew thicker and more dwarfish as we ascended, till they became mere shrubs, and literally matted together so that you could not see two feet in advance of you. Through, and over these we floundered, and urged our steps; yet, tired as I was, I could not but stop and laugh to see B——n fight his way through. Rolling himself over like a cart-wheel, he would disappear in the thick evergreens; in a short time his face, red with the fierce struggle, would rise like that of a spent swimmer's over the waves; and then with a crash he went out of sight again; and so kept up the battle for at least half an hour. Here we passed over the bed of a moose, which we doubtless roused from his repose, for the rank grass was still matted where he had lain. At length we emerged upon the brow of a cliff, across a gulf at the base of which arose a bare, naked pyramid, that pushed its rocky forehead high into the heavens. This was the summit of Tahawus. A smooth, gray rock, shaped like an inverted bowl, stood before us, as if on purpose to mock all our efforts. Half-way up this was S——th, looking no larger than a dog, as with his pack on his back he crawled on all fours over the rocks. Hitherto nothing could knock the fun out of him; and as he from time to time stumbled on a log, or heard the complaint of some one behind, he would sing, in a comical sort of a chorus, '*go-in-up*,' followed by his hearty ha-ha-ha, as if he were impervious to fatigue. To every hallo we sent after him, he would return that everlasting '*go-in-up*,' sung out so funnily that we invariably echoed back his laugh, till the mountains rang again. But now he was silent, the '*go-in-up*' had become a serious matter, and it required all his breath to enable him to 'go up.'

"As we ascended this bald cone, the chill wind swept by like a December blast, and well it might, for the snow had been gone but a few weeks. The fir-trees had gradually dwindled away, till they were not taller than your finger, and now disappeared altogether; for nothing but naked rock could resist the climate of this high region. The dogs, which had hitherto scoured the forest on every side, crouched close and shivering to our side, — evidently frightened, as they looked off on empty space, — and all was dreary, savage, and wild.

"At length we reached the top; and oh, what a view spread out before, or rather below us. Here we were, more than a mile high in the heavens, on the highest point of land in the Empire State; and with one exception the highest in the Union; and in the centre of a chaos of mountains, the like of which I never saw before. It was wholly different from the Alps. There were no snow peaks and shining glaciers; but all was gray, or green, or black, as far as the vision could extend. It looked as if the Almighty had once set this vast earth rolling like the sea; and then, in the midst of its maddest flow, bid all the gigantic billows stop and congeal in their places. And there they stood just as He froze them — grand and gloomy. There was the long swell, and there the cresting, bursting billow, and there the deep, black, cavernous gulf. Far away — more than fifty miles to the south-east — a storm was raging, and the massive clouds over the distant mountains of Vermont, or rather *between* us and them, and below their summits, stood balanced in space, with their white tops towering over their black and dense bases, as if they were the margin of Jehovah's mantle folded back to let the earth beyond be seen. That far-away storm against a background of mountains, and with nothing but the most savage scenery between — how mysterious, how awful it seemed!

" Mount Colden, with its terrific precipices, — Mount McIntyre, with its bold, black, monster-like head, — White Face, with its white spot on its forehead, and countless other summits, pierced the heavens in every direction. And then, such a stretch of forest, for more than three hundred miles in circumference, — ridges and slopes of green, broken only by lakes that dared just to peep into view from their deep hiding-places, — one vast wilderness seamed here and there by a river whose surface you could not see, but whose course you could follow by the black winding gap through the tops of the trees. Still there was beauty as well as grandeur in the scene. Lake Champlain, with its islands, spread away as far as the eye could follow towards the Canadas, while the distant Green Mountains rolled their granite summits along the eastern horizon, with Burlington curtained in smoke at their feet. To the north-west gleamed out here and there the lakes of the Saranac River, and farther to the west those of the Raquette; nearer by, Lake Sanford, Placid Lake, Lake Colden, Lake Henderson, shine in quiet beauty amid the solitude. Nearly thirty lakes in all were visible, — some dark as polished jet, beneath the shadow of girdling mountains; others flashing out upon the limitless landscape, like smiles to relieve the gloom of the great solitude. Throughout the wide extent but three clearings were visible — all was as Nature made it. My head swam in the wondrous vision, and I seemed lifted up above the earth and shown all its mountains and forests and lakes at once. But the impression of the whole it is impossible to convey, — nay, I am myself hardly conscious what it is. It seems as if I had seen vagueness, terror, sublimity, strength, and beauty, all embodied, so that I had a new and more definite knowledge of them. God appears to have wrought in these old mountains with His highest power, and designed to leave a symbol of His omnipotence. Man is nothing here; his very shouts die on his lips. One of our company tried to sing, but his voice fled from him into the empty space. We fired a gun, but it gave only half a report, and no echo came back, for there was nothing to check the sound in its flight. 'God is great,' is the language of the heart, as it swells over such a scene."

"Clouds are rolling around him to-day," says Mr. Headley, speaking of Mount Tahawus on a later occasion, "and I think of what Professor Benedict, of Burlington, told me. He ascended it once for scientific purposes, and made experiments on the top, which have been of great service to the State. He said that the spectacle from it, one morning in a north-east storm, was sublime beyond description. He was in the clear sunlight, while an ocean of clouds rolled on below him in vast white undulations, blotting out the whole creation from his view. At length, under the influence of the sun, this limitless deep slowly rent asunder, and the black top of a mountain slowly emerged like an island from the mighty mass, and then another and another, till away, for more than three hundred miles in circumference, these black conical islands were sprinkled over the white bosom of the vapory sea. The lower portions of the mountains then appeared, while the mist collected in the deep gulfs, and lay like a vast serpent over the bed of a river, that wound through the forest below, or shot up into fantastic shapes resembling towers and domes and cliffs, and clouds frowning and shifting and changing in bewildering confusion. It is impossible to conceive anything half so strange and wild."

> " Oh, it was an unimaginable sight:
> Clouds, mists, streams, waters, rock, and emerald turf;
> Clouds of all tincture, rocks, and sapphire sky,
> Confused, commingled, mutually inflamed,
> Molten together, and composing thus,
> Each lost in each, a marvellous array
> Of temple, palace, citadel, and huge
> Fantastic pomp of structure without name,
> In fleecy folds voluminous enwrapped.

Such by the Hebrew prophets were beheld
In vision — forms uncouth of mightiest power,
For admiration and mysterious awe."

Pages might be written concerning the mountains of this region, but they would hardly differ from each other enough to justify us in writing them, so much does one peak resemble another in its skyey outlook and the landscapes around its base. The Indian Pass, however, a noted mountain-scene here about, being an exception to the general rule, must not be passed over without description. Its chief characteristics may be gathered from the following lines of Bryant, who in writing them had a different view before him, — that of Monument Mountain, a remarkable precipice in the western part of Massachusetts.

" There is a precipice
That seems a fragment of some mighty wall,
Built by the hand that fashioned the old world,
To separate its nations, and thrown down
When the flood drowned them. To the north, a path
Conducts you up the narrow battlement.
Steep is the western side, shaggy and wild
With mossy trees, and pinnacles of flint,
And many a hanging crag. But, to the east,
Sheer to the vale go down the bare old cliffs, —
Huge pillars, that in middle heavens upbear
Their weather-beaten capitals, here dark
With moss, the growth of centuries, and there
Of chalky whiteness where the thunderbolt
Has splintered them. It is a fearful thing
To stand upon the beetling verge, and see
Where storm and lightning, from that huge gray wall,

Have tumbled down vast blocks, and at the base
Dashed them in fragments, and to lay thine ear
Over the dizzy depths, and hear the sound
Of winds, that struggle with the woods below,
Come up like ocean murmurs. But the scene
Is lovely round; a beautiful river there
Wanders amid the fresh and fertile meads,
The paradise He made unto Himself,
Mining the soil for ages. On each side
The fields swell upward to the hills; beyond,
Above the hills, in the blue distance, rise
The mountain columns with which earth props heaven."

The Indian Pass was visited by Mr. Headley, by whom it is thus described. " I had expected, from paintings I had seen of this Pass, that I was to walk almost on a level into a huge gap between two mountains, and look up on the precipices that toppled heaven-high above me. But here was a world of rocks overgrown with trees and moss, over and under and between which we were compelled to crawl and dive and work our way with so much exertion and care that the strongest soon began to be exhausted. Caverns opened on every side; and a more hideous, toilsome, breakneck tramp I never took. Leaping a chasm at one time, we paused upon the brow of an overhanging cliff, while Cheney, pointing below, said, ' There, I've scared panthers from those caverns many times; we may meet one yet; if so, I think he 'll remember us as *long as he lives!* ' I thought the probabilities were, that we should remember *him* much longer than he would us. At least I had no desire to task his memory, being perfectly willing to leave the matter unde-

cided. There was a stream somewhere ; but no foot could follow it, for it was a succession of cascades, with perpendicular walls each side hemming it in. It was more like climbing a broken and shattered mountain than entering a gorge. At length, however, we came where the fallen rocks had made an open space around and spread a fearful ruin in their place. On many of these, trees were growing fifty feet high, while a hundred men could find shelter in their sides. As the eye sweeps over these fragments of a former earthquake, the imagination is busy with the past — the period when an interlocking range of mountains was riven, and the encircling peaks bowing in terror, reeled like ships upon a tossing ocean, and the roar of a thousand storms rolled away from the yawning gulf, into which precipices and forests went down with the deafening crash of a falling world. A huge mass that had then been loosened from its high bed and hurled below, making a cliff of itself, from which to fall would have been certain death, our guide called the ' Church,' — and it did lift itself there like a huge altar, right in front of the main precipice that rose in a naked wall, more than a thousand feet perpendicular. It is two thousand feet from the summit to the base; but part of the chasm has been filled with its own ruins, so that the spot on which you stand is a thousand feet above the valley below, and nearly three thousand above tide-water. Thus it stretches for three quarters of a mile ; in no place less than five hundred feet perpendicular. By dint of scrambling and pulling each other up, we at last succeeded in reaching the top of the 'Church,' while from our very feet rose this very cliff that really oppressed us with its near and frightful presence. Majestic, solemn, and silent, with the daylight from above pouring all over its dread form, it stood the impersonation of strength and grandeur."

It is not for its mountains and forests alone, however, that the Wilderness of Northern New York is remarkable, for these might be paralleled to some extent elsewhere; not so its multitude of waters, countless lakes reflecting the sky in their crystal mirrors, and numberless streams threading their way through the shadowy recesses of the woods. One of the former, lying in the heart of the Adirondacks, is thus described by Mr. Headley. "It is the largest body of water in this wild region, and with a shore as irregular as it could well be made. Though only thirteen miles long and six broad, it has a coast of *fifty miles in extent.* With its long wooded points and promontories and deep bays, it would look, to a man placed above it, like a huge scallop. This waving outline completely deceives one, in sailing over it, as to the extent and direction of the main body of water. As you round one point, the lake seems to take a turn, for it goes miles away piercing the very heart of the distant forest. But by the time a second point is weathered, a broad and beautiful surface is seen spreading in another direction. Thus there is a constant succession of new views; in fact, as you slowly float along, you seem to behold a dozen different lakes, each rivalling the other in picturesque beauty. It has three large inlets, one of which comes from the Eckford, or, as the hunters call them, Blue Mountain and Tallow Lakes, pouring a stream of crystal into its bosom. The south inlet is a river of such magnitude that it can be navigated for eight miles by a boat of a ton's burden. The third is Brown's Inlet, of almost half the size of the former.

"Imagine this broad expanse of water in the midst of a vast wilderness, dotted with islands, with deep bays fringed with green; bold slopes reaching to the clouds, clothed with green; distant mountains, enfolding mountains, all waving with the same rich verdure; blue peaks, dreaming far away and far up in the heavens, — and not a sign of vegetation, not a boat to break the solitude, — and you will have some idea of the sights that meet you at every turn, charming the soul into pleasure."

The portion of the wilderness which has been most written about is the region watered by the Saranac and Racket rivers and lakes, — a wild and picturesque country, which Mr. Street has made the subject of a volume descriptive of a summer jaunt therein. It abounds in glowing descriptions of woods and waters, as witness this picture of the Saranac River.

"Directly at the entrance, on our right, lay an expanse of wild grass and thickets, with a deep fringing of water-plants.

"The views now changed suddenly as the scenes of a theatre. The banks became low, the woods frequently yielding to broad spaces of natural grass, called indifferently by the guides, parks and wild meadows. They were skirted, next the water, either with thickets or trees, the green levels beyond being seen through the loops and vistas of the foliage.

" Sometimes these meadows wound like bays into the recesses of the background forest, beckoning the fancy to distant nooks of beauty.

" Here and there in the forked head of a dry tree was the nest of the fish-hawk, a rounded mass of gray withered sticks. From the abundance of the water in these woods, this bird haunts almost every scene, and its huge nest, frequently met, gives a wild picturesqueness to the monotony of the verdure.

" Spread over the shallows was a broad floor of lily-pads, glistening in green varnish, and brilliant with white and yellow blossoms, the pearly scallops of the former resting on the surface, and the globes of the latter erect upon their short thick stems.

" The dark-red Mohawk-tassel and the scarlet-berried Solomon's-seal gleamed upon the banks, and on their tall stems, tufted in the water, shone the purple-blossomed moose-head.

" Between these meadows, the forest thronged to the river's edge so densely as to slant many of the skirting trees nearly athwart the stream. We skimmed over the shadows in the water, where some jagged branch was so accurately depicted it seemed that the little bluebird would be torn while gliding over.

LANDSCAPE AND POETRY.

"Black, soaking logs, almost buried in the water-weeds, lay along or pointed from the banks, whence the twittering stream-birds vanished at our approach, while from among the plants, the duck whizzed and the frog and occasional musk-rat plunged."

Still more picturesque, at least in details, is Mr. Street's description of the scenery along the banks of Racket River.

"Past the bald hemlock flowing with moss like an old bearded prophet; past the ruined elm, its top tilting to our ripple and raising dimples in the water; past the gray finger of the skeleton pine, — finger pointing to the centuries that have rolled over the forest; past the water-maple's peristyle of pillars upholding the blended dome; past the ledge green with moss as an emerald; past the tongues of the banks thrust far out into the channel, and the coves of hollowed foliage where the duck dimly seen had doubtless cast anchor for the day; past the red oak hardened into iron like the trees of Járnvids, and wreathed into green softness by the moss; past the trunk wrestling on the border with some straggling grape-vine, a Laocoon of the wood; past the windy bubbles in the channel where the rain launched its fiercest lash, we swept along. On either hand frowned the aboriginal wilderness, — wilderness like that which walled Hudson as he tracked up his river; which darkened on Champlain as he coasted down his lake; where no axe but the one clearing space for the shanty had ever rung, no smoke had ever curled save that breathed by the camp-fire; close-twined save at the beautiful green openings, grassy nests of the forest, tempting one to make there a home where existence should glide along in sylvan peace.

"Down we went over the glossy greens, the glittering whites of the river; down past elms and spruces, and hemlocks and pines, and water-maples and alders; down past sandbanks and gravel beds, sunken logs and slanting trees; old withered upright trees, and trees thrust midway into the channel where the water eddied and sparkled; down past lily-pads and water-grasses, leafy arcades and cloisters, colonnades and peeping nooks; down past glades and swamps and lichened ledges and dry ridges brown with the dropped needles of the pine:

"Down the winding woodland river,
 Oh how swift we glide!
Every tree and bush and blossom
 Mirrored in the tide;
Bright and blue the heaven above us
 As — whose azure eye!
Soft and sweet the wandering breezes
 As — whose gentle sigh!
While the cloudlet wreathing o'er us
 As her spotless brow!
Oh what king was e'er so joyous
 As we roamers now!
 Ho, ho, we merrily go
  Down the winding sparkling flow!
  Down so cheerily,
  Never wearily,
 Ho, ho, we merrily go
 Down to the lovely lake below!

"Mark the crane wide winnowing from us;
　　Off the otter skims!
　Round her fortress sails the fish-hawk;
　　Down the wood-duck swims!
　Glitters rich the golden lily,
　　Glows the Indian Plume;
　On yon point a deer is drinking,
　　Back he shrinks in gloom;
　Now the little sparkling rapid!
　Now the fairy cove!
　Here, the sunlight-mantled meadow!
　　There, the sprinkled grove!
　　　Ho, ho, we merrily go
　　　Down the winding glittering flow!
　　　　Down so cheerily,
　　　　Never wearily,
　　　Ho, ho, we merrily go
　　　Down to the lovely lake below!"

As we have confined ourselves hitherto to the outward life of the Wilderness,— the forms of its landscapes, the aspect of its woods, waters, and mountains, — let us now glance at some of its myriads of living creatures, or rather let Mr. Street do so for us. He is looking at a pool.

"In its airlike depth was a trout, moving around restlessly, scenting a lily-stem; pondering over a mossy rock; darting toward the surface; steadying himself by the occasional flutter of his f is; staring with huge eyes all about; waving his tail, like a deer grazing, and working his mouth as if chewing a cud. By-and-by a miller came close to the glass of the surface, quivering with admiration at the image of his silver coat. His spasm of self-love was short, for the trout, lurking in the ambush of a stone, like a bandit in his cave, darted forth, gave a nip, and the luckless miller vanished.

"Then came a shiner that sent a flash through all the pool. Now he poised himself, head downwards, as if to lunge through the ooze; then stood on his tail and gaped. At last he turned himself into a wheel and gyrated away. He was succeeded by a gleam of gold, cast by a sunfish that flattened himself on his side and lay there until a bull-head blundered along and turned one of his horns on him, when the sunfish whisked himself away.

"At this juncture there was a plump, and then a sudden darkening of the crystal enclosure, through which I saw the dim shape of a musk-rat, who scampered across the bottom, and then rose by a sedge on a dot of grass, with its flag half-way up its staff.

"First, his ratship pulled the stem of a yellow lily, as if to ring the bell; then he nibbled the gold off the blossom; then he skimmed to the edge of the bank, with two furrows like a wedge pencilled from his shoulders, and cut with his needle-teeth the barb of an arrow-head, and towed it with his mouth to his burrow, where he vanished. In a moment, however, his blunt, whiskered face and glittering specks of eyes were thrust forth again in my direction, thinking, I suppose, what a queer thing that log was, when an involuntary motion on my part caused him to disappear in the winking of an eye."

It is not with "such small deer" as these, however, that the Wilderness is mostly peopled, and for which it is so attractive to sportsmen, but game of another sort, chief among which is, of course, the deer, the most poetical, as it certainly is the most graceful, of all the forest animals. A description of the deer and its habits would make a charming paper, but unfortunately it does not come within the scope of this chapter, which is already, we fear, too long; we close it therefore with a hunting-song, in which the theme lingers as the sound of a bugle in the echoes of a mountain. It is from the pen of Mr. Street.

"The woods are all sleeping, the midnight is dark;
We launch on the still wave our bubble-like bark;
The rifle all ready, the jack burning clear,
And we brush through the lily-pads, floating for deer;
   Floating for deer;
As we glide o'er the shallows, boys, floating for deer.

"We turn the low meadow; now breathless we skim;
That eye! no, the phosphor! yon head! no, a limb!
This step in the stream! no, a spring dripping near!
Thus we brush through the lily-pads, floating for deer;
   Floating for deer;
Thus we glide o'er the shallows, boys, floating for deer.

"Yon nook! spring the locks! the deer's eyeballs of fire!
Still, still as a shadow! hush! nigher, yet nigher!
Crack, splash! draw him in! now away in good cheer,
Through the lily-pads blithely from floating for deer;
   Floating for deer;
Back to camp, through the shallow, from floating for deer."

CHAPTER IV.

FLORA AND FAUNA.

The Fauna and Flora of the settled portion of the Wilderness being such as are common to the latitude and the State generally, and consequently of a familiar character, stand in no need of description. As they present, however, in the wilder regions some peculiar features, it may not be amiss to devote a few pages to the latter. As might be expected from the natural configuration of the country, — its vast forests, its steep and wooded mountains, and its lack of human inhabitants, — wild animals, as bears and panthers, abound, and the fur-bearing tribes — the Sable, the Fisher, and the Beaver.

The most remarkable, perhaps, of the larger animals is the Moose, so called from the Indian word "Mussee," signifying wood-eater, and which is known to zoölogists as the *Cervus Alces*, and is variously styled the American Elk, the Black Elk, the Moose Deer, etc. In stature the moose is large, with a long head, narrowed before the eyes, and enlarged into a thick, curved nose. The nostrils are long, the muzzle small. The eyes, which are moderately large, are placed near the base of the horns;

the ears are long, while the neck is very short, and is furnished with a short mane. The horns occur only in the male. The color of the moose is a dark gray, and the size equals that of an average horse. It is remarkably awkward and ungainly in its movements; its habits are marked and distinctive. In summer it haunts the streams and lakes, feeding upon aquatic plants, especially the pond-lily. It devours grasses and twigs of trees, and is particularly fond of the striped white maple, which from this circumstance is sometimes called " moose-wood." It is also addicted to peeling old trees, and lunching off their bark. In the cold season the moose herd together in the woods. They are very shy, and, in spite of their awkwardness, very fleet; the sense of hearing and smelling are so acute in them that hunters consider it a great achievement to kill a moose. Their hide furnishes the material for good moccasins and snow-shoes, and their flesh is very palatable; when young, it is hardly distinguishable from veal; the nose and tongue are considered the choicest morsels. The moose, when young, is said to be capable of domestication, and has even been used for agricultural purposes. Racket Lake was formerly a great settlement of these animals, which are becoming more and more scarce; in a short time they will probably disappear.

The Wolverine is found here. It has a short, compact body, with an arched back, a little raised from the ground; a small, broad, rounded head, with small ears nearly hidden in fur. The eyes are small, the fur loose and shaggy, the tail short and bushy, the legs thick and short, with clawed feet. The color varies from a light cream to a deep, dark brown. It is a troublesome and mischievous animal, destroying traps, etc. It is seldom if ever found, we believe, south of Racket Lake.

Deer are as numerous as dogs in more civilized localities. The fox, the wolf, the marten, the hare, the lynx, the otter, the wild-cat, the racoon, and the minx are found more or less frequently. The Indians have traditions of a strange and ferocious animal, called the Yagesho, which flourished here centuries ago, and which has long been extinct: most naturalists deny that it ever existed.

The ornithology of the Wilderness embraces the birds common to the State and latitude, besides various species peculiar to the bleaker regions of the country.

The Canada Jay breeds around the sources of the Saranac. This species has a leaden-gray back; its hind head is black, its forehead, collar, and tip of the tail, dusky white. The plumage is loose, and the length varies from ten to twelve inches. It seems to be omnivorous, devouring berries, eggs of other birds, and even carrion.

In the spruce-forests is found a species of grouse which is generally known as the Spruce Grouse. It is sub-crested, darkish, spotted with white. The tail is rounded, with brownish-red tips, and the throat and breast are black. This bird is also known as the Canada Grouse, and the Spruce Partridge. In spite of its suggestive name, however, the flesh is not very edible, having a bitter taste.

The raven is sometimes seen here. It is omnivorous, and common alike to Europe and America.

The Arctic Woodpecker is found in various localities. It has a yellow crown, with a white band stretching from the mandible and passing under the eye; the outer tail-feathers are white and rufous. The female is without the yellow crown. This bird abounds in the forests of Herkimer and Hamilton counties in June, and has also been found at Niagara. It breeds here, and feeds on the tree-boring insects.

The American Swan is found in the lonelier districts; as the uninhabited portions of Hamilton and Herkimer counties, and around the outlet of Tupper's Lake. This species was shown by Dr. Sharpless to be distinct from the swan of Europe.

The birds, however, which possess the most interest for the general reader, are the Eagle and the Loon. Naturalists divide the genus Eagle into two species. The first of these, the Golden Eagle, (*Aquila Chrysætos,*) is a rare bird. It is solitary in its habits, a pair seeming to monopolize a district. It builds its nest in inaccessible rocky peaks, devouring birds and quadrupeds, but never touching aught that is dead. The second, the Brown or Bald Eagle, is found all over the United States. It feeds on fish, wild-fowl, and small quadrupeds; pursues and conquers the fish-hawk, and builds its nest on lofty trees.

The Loon is a remarkable bird, and has been much written of by visitors to the Adirondack region. It is thus described by Mr. Street in his *Woods and Waters.* "As the boat glided downward, I looked again and again at the dark purple-green of the loon's neck; the two white collars below; his back and wings of ebony, inlaid with pearl; the pure snow of his undershape; the black dagger of his beak; his fierce, red eye; and his short, straight, jointless leg, so adapted to propel the buoyant bark of his body. His structure was wild, almost grotesque, and like his Indian whoop, was in harmony with the secluded and savage waters which he alone makes his home." The cry of the loon is a most peculiar sound, and once heard is not readily forgotten. It has been described as the laugh of a maniac, or rather the jeering laugh of a demon over a fallen victim, — a bitter, taunting laugh and yell mingled. The loon is emphatically an aquatic bird. It often appears on the surface of a lake as a mere black speck, and as it dives with wonderful rapidity it is a very difficult bird to kill. The saying, "crazy as a loon," originated from the maniacal whoop of this singular creature.

A species of nightingale, known as the Saranac Nightingale, is found in the Wilderness region; and the loud, clear, triumphal music of its voice rises above the shriek of the eagle, the croak of the raven, the boom of the bittern, and the shouting of the loon. Flocks of wild pigeons containing hundreds of thousands are frequently to be seen.

On the reptiles of the region we need not dwell particularly. The rattlesnake is found in certain quarters, the

FLORA AND FAUNA. 59

wood-terrapin, and other species of creeping things. The fish for which the waters hereabout are most noted is the trout. It is of three varieties: the Small Trout, the Speckled Trout, and the Lake Trout.

The Flora of the Northern Botanical District of New York embraces not only the ordinary plants of level and cultivated regions of corresponding latitude, but, in its more mountainous regions, an Alpine vegetation.

On the higher peaks are found, among others, the following plants. The Alpine Willow Herb, the common European Golden Rod, and the Procumbent Alpine Rosebay. The latter, which grows on the loftiest mountain summits, is to be met with on the White Hills of New Hampshire, and is common to the Western Continent. The Alpine Bilberry, loving the rocky clefts; the Lapland Daphensia, peculiar to high latitudes and localities; the Meadow Grass, the Alpine Holy-Grass, a rare species; the purple Alpine Hair-Grass, a curious grass, identical with the Lapland plant of the same name; the Crow-berry, the Slender Fringed Rush, the Sedge, and other plants peculiar to high mountains of the northern hemisphere, or natives of the Arctic Zone.

Another plant common to the region is the Water-lily, of which there are two kinds, the white and the yellow. They grow from an immense rough stem, several feet in length, embedded in the bottom. This throws out fibres, which, lengthening, lets up the bud to blossom on the surface. The water-lily is a favorite food with the deer.

CHAPTER V.

GEOLOGY, MINERALOGY, IRON, LUMBER, AGRICULTURAL RESOURCES, COMMERCE, MANUFACTURES, ETC.

The nine counties of which the region is composed lie in what is scientifically termed the Second and Third Geological Districts of New York. The former embraces the counties of Warren, Essex, Clinton, Franklin, St. Lawrence, Jefferson, and Hamilton; the latter, those of Herkimer and Lewis.

The Second Geological District may be regarded as an insulated portion of the State bordered by three valleys, — those of the Champlain, Mohawk, and St. Lawrence rivers. It is traversed by ranges of mountains, whose arrangement, though seemingly irregular, is in reality sufficiently regular. Its valleys are few, and, being long and narrow, partake of the character of gorges.

Their number and direction is determined by the rivers laid down on the map.

The District in many parts is elevated, as may be seen by the following table of some of its heights above the tide.

Tupper and Cranberry Lakes, ...	1500 feet.
Saranac Lakes, ...	1500 "

GEOLOGY, MINERALOGY, IRON, LUMBER, ETC. 61

Lake Sanford,	1826 feet
Adirondack Iron Works	1889 "
Lake Colden	2851 "
Mount Whiteface	4000 "
Mount Seward	5100 "
Dix's Peak	5200 "
Mount Marcy	5467 "

In Warren County the rocks are chiefly primary. The main rock is gneiss. Limestone, serpentine, and peat not unfrequently occur. The great feature of Essex County is the abundance of the hypersthene rock, rising as it were in the centre of mountains, and joining the nucleus around which all other rocks are dispersed. The veins of iron in this county are another important feature. Primary limestone exists in large quantities, while the sedimentary rocks and the tertiary formation exhibit some interesting scientific phenomena. The igneous and trap rocks are comparatively few. The Adirondack Mountains are a prominent element in the landscape, and the celebrated Adirondack Pass is as interesting geologically as it is poetically sublime. The trap-dyke at Avalanche Lake is also a curious spectacle. Clinton County is rich in iron; the ores are in veins. The chief geological feature is the development of the lower members of what is called "The New York System of Rocks." The primary rocks are granite and gneiss. The greatest development takes place in the lower limestones. The rocks abound in fossils. There is also much "drift." The curious features presented by the phenomena of the loose materials, etc. of this county, support the belief that it was elevated from a submersion by several successive uplifts. In Franklin County the primary rocks predominate. St. Lawrence County embraces three geological divisions: the region of primary rocks, that of sandstone, and that of limestone. This county contains much specular iron ore. Jefferson County is strongly marked by diluvial action. The rocks are not irregularly arranged, and much of the soil is suited for agricultural purposes. Hamilton County is wild and rocky. Its principal feature is the abundance of its lakes. The same may be said of Herkimer County. Of Lewis County, the last of the series, the geology presents nothing that demands special notice.

The region contains a variety of mineral springs, as Nitrogen, Sulphur, and what are denominated "Petrifying Springs." Thus we have the Chateaugay Springs, in Franklin County; the Essex County Springs, and Sulphur Springs, at Beekman, Clinton County; and at several localities in St. Lawrence County calcareous tufa is deposited from springs in St. Lawrence and Franklin counties; and a remarkable deposit of the same nature is found near the head of Otsego Creek, in Herkimer County.

Copper is found in considerable quantities throughout St. Lawrence County and elsewhere, while large deposits of Galena, or Sulphuret of Lead, have been discovered in various sections of the region. Mines of this last metal have been worked at different times with various degrees of success, as the Rossie Lead Mine, the Robinson, Ross, and Jepson mines, and though they did not at the time fulfil the perhaps too sanguine expectations of their projectors, they are destined, we believe, to prove a profitable investment to skilful capitalists.

Serpentine is also found in the region. This fine green stone, so beautiful by nature, and so susceptible of polish by art, is valuable as a marble, and should be used more extensively than at present. Mixed with granular limestone, it forms the celebrated Verd Antique. Serpentine is found in other portions of the State, but so impure that it is of no practical utility. But the Serpentine of Northern New York, especially that of St. Lawrence County, is of excellent quality, and only needs the requisite facilities of transportation to become an important product.

Associated with Serpentine in St. Lawrence County is Soapstone. In consequence of being soft and tenacious, this stone can be moulded, and then rendered hard by exposure to heat. It is a useful article, and can be made yet more valuable commercially. Clays of every variety are not wanting in the region, while its resources of Marble are comparatively unknown and untouched. St. Lawrence County contains an abundance of White Limestone, and Water Limestones are found in other localities. Marl exists in St. Lawrence County; and in Essex County there are large quantities of Graphite, (Plumbago, or Black Lead).

The most important product of the region, however, is Iron, which is found in nearly every county therein. In

Essex and Clinton counties it is especially abundant. In the former may be mentioned the Penfield ore-bed, the Cragharbor ore, the Cheever Mine, near Port Henry, the Sanford Mine, in the town of Moriah, about six miles west of Port Henry, the Barnum Mine, Hale's Mine, the Everett Mine, and others.

The largest deposits of iron in Essex County are in the town of Newcomb, and are known as the Sanford Mine. This mine is placed on the western face of a hill overlooking Lake Sanford, about ten miles from the village of McIntyre.

In Clinton County is found the Arnold Bed, which contains a vast quantity of good iron. The whole county, in fact, is very rich in mineral capabilities. Iron has also been discovered in Herkimer County.

The iron principally exists in the form of Magnetic Oxide, though the Specular Oxide also exists. St. Lawrence County is rich in this latter product, as in what are called the Kearney and Parish ore-beds. This form of iron is also found in other counties. What is known as Bog Iron ore abounds in St. Lawrence County; indeed, there is scarcely a town within its limits in which this variety of iron does not occur.

Magnetic deposits are found at Oakham, Harewood, Sherwood, and elsewhere. The Iron Mountain at Oakham was discovered in 1852. It furnishes an inexhaustible supply of the best quality of iron. This remark applies also to the veins at Harewood, Sherwood, Grandshue, and Clifton. The Clifton ore-bed is especially rich.

Professor Emmons wrote years ago of the Newcomb or Adirondack ore-bed as follows : — " In order to obtain a correct conception of the amount of ore on the Sanford Hill, we may estimate its solid contents ; or if we merely estimate the amount of ore at the depth of two feet from the surface, we shall find that it amounts to at least 6,832,737 tons, a large proportion of which may be removed or raised without the use of power. This amount of ore will produce at least 3,000,000 tons of iron of the best quality." Again he remarks : " There probably never was a vein so favorably situated, and where so little capital will be required to obtain the ore and transport it to the place where it is to be reduced. A very remarkable fact observable in relation to the Sanford vein, is its entire freedom from pyrites, and any other substances known to exert an injurious effect on iron. In fact the ore of the vein is one of the purest which is at present known, if we except the Arnold ore." In another place he says : " Such at any rate I conceive to be the qualities of the iron, that it is a matter of national importance that the operations in its manufacture should be conducted in the best possible mode. There are some particular uses to which this iron can be applied, and for which there is nothing equal to it made in this country."

The following anecdote is related in reference to the original Adirondack iron-bed. "An Indian approached the late David Henderson, Esq., of Jersey City, in the year 1826, whilst standing near the Elba Iron Works, and taking from beneath his blanket a piece of iron ore, he presented it to Mr. H. with the inquiry, expressed in his imperfect English, 'You want to see 'um ore? me find plenty, all same.' When asked where it came from, he pointed to the southwest, and exclaimed, ' Me hunt beaver all 'lone, and find 'um where water run over iron dam.'

"The Indian proved to be a brave of the St. Francis tribe, honest, quiet, and intelligent, who spent the summers in hunting amid the wilds of the Adirondack. An exploring party was promptly arranged, who, submitting themselves to the guidance of the Indian, plunged into the pathless forest. The first night they made their bivouac beneath the giant walls of the Indian Pass. The next day they reached the site of the present works, and there saw the strange spectacle described by the brave: the actual flow of the river over an iron dam, created by a ledge of ore, which formed a barrier across the stream.

"The reconnoissance revealed to their astonished view various and immense deposits of ore, equal almost to the demands of the world for ages.

"A glance disclosed the combination, in that secluded spot, of all the ingredients, and every facility for the most extensive manufacture of iron, in all its departments. In close proximity existed an illimitable supply of ore, boundless forests of hard wood, and an abundant water-power. The remote position of the locality formed the chief impediment to the scheme which was at once adopted by the intelligent explorers."

Not deterred by this consideration, they immediately secured the purchase of an extensive tract of over a million of acres, embracing not only the entire Adirondack ore-beds, but also water-power, wood, and limestone lands sufficient for the working of the ores for generations. A road was constructed to the site, a settlement was commenced, iron was produced equal to the best Swedish ores, and the proprietors, Messrs. McIntyre, Robertson, and Henderson, displayed the greatest energy. Professor Emmons, as State Geologist, visited this region for five years, and in 1842 made an elaborate Report to the State, extracts from which have already been quoted. The length of this Report prevents its insertion entire, but it is well worth perusal. It enters fully into all points regarding the quantity and other important characteristics of the ores, treats of the Sanford ore, the coarse-grained or black ore, the fine-grained ore, and other beds and varieties. Professor Johnson also furnished a Report upon the iron of the region, in which he speaks of the ores in the highest terms known to practical science.

Stimulated by these Reports, the State of New York caused a survey of the Valley of the Upper Hudson to be made, with reference to the construction of a canal. The project, however, was finally abandoned, much to the disappointment of McIntyre and his associates. At last, (though their ore commanded a far higher price than any other,) owing to the expenses of its long overland transportation, these gentlemen were compelled to suspend operations temporarily. But in the mean time their attention had been turned to the peculiar fitness of their iron for conversion into steel; and in 1848, they, with other parties, organized the Adirondack Iron and Steel Company, at Jersey City, N. J. James R. Thompson, Esq., the superintendent of these works, proves conclusively in his Report (1854), that the Adirondack iron furnishes a first-class quality of steel, equal to the best Swedish iron. Testimonies as to the quality of this iron have been received from the highest sources. At the World's Fair in London, the jury awarded the Company a gold medal for a specimen of its iron and steel.

There can be no doubt that everything is favorable to the development of the iron wealth of Northern New York, when it shall have proper facilities for transportation. There is absolutely no lack of material — no limit to it. The iron seems to be literally inexhaustible, capable of supplying the demands of centuries yet to come, while the quality is as fine as the quantity is vast, far surpassing in kind the ores of more southern regions. Wood is abundant, and thus an important element in iron-manufacture is supplied. The timber, like the iron, cannot fail while the lakes and streams of the region afford a plenteous supply of water-power for the working of all necessary machinery. In short, all that is needed for the prosecution of successful mining enterprise is individual exertion. Nature has done her work, let man fulfil his part. Let him labor and prosper.

The timber of the region likewise demands a share of attention as well as the iron. Millions of acres of woodland exist here, which in years to come will be forced to yield their riches to Trade and Commerce, although at present they stand dark, dense, primeval, poetical, — and useless. In certain portions a considerable amount of lumbering is done, but as a general rule the timber facilities of the region are utterly neglected. But all this will be changed in time; railroads and canals will bring the Wilderness within reach of civilization, and the lumberman will take the place of the hunter.

Pine, hemlock, cedar, spruce, fir, maple, beech, birch, moose-wood, bass-wood, ash, walnut, sugar-maple, tamarack, and other woods, are scattered throughout the forest. The bird's-eye and curled-grain maple, with the elegant mottled birch, are of such a quality that in the hands of a skilful cabinet-maker they might be made to supersede mahogany and rosewood. The spruce, larch, and tamarack grow to a great size, and are in demand for decking, and spars as well as boards. Among the "soft woods," are pines varying from ninety to one hundred and twenty feet in height, without a limb; in diameter sufficient, and in quality suitable, for the masts of our clipper ships, or for the main shafts of our largest factories. Various approximate estimates have been made of the average value per acre of the forest in different parts of the region. The following is from the "Forest Arcadia."

"Mr. Thomas McCaw, who, several years ago, made a critical examination of a large portion of its area, and whose judgment is beyond question, makes this estimate of the quantities of material to be found upon one acre, as a mean of the forest, namely: thirty cords of merchantable wood; one spar of 128 cubic feet (as a mean);

five cords of hemlock bark; 2280 feet, board measure, of pine lumber; 13,680 feet, board measure, of spruce, hemlock, etc.; 6840 feet, maple, birch, beech; and the mean net value per acre to be $201." Of another section of this region another writer says: "In fine, so great is the growth of this whole forest, that were it felled and cut up into cord-wood, it would average upon each and every acre 75 cords. Below is the general average (on one acre) of a series of estimates made at different parts of this forest during the prosecution of the survey, namely:

2000 feet (board measure) spruce.
1000   "   "   "   pine.
4000   "   "   "   hemlock.
2000   "   "   "   maple.
1500   "   "   "   birch.
1500   "   "   "   beech.
1000   "   "   "   various woods.

2½ cords of hemlock bark, and 50 cords of merchantable wood, or 2500 bushels of charcoal."

Other estimates place the value of the forest per acre even higher than those already given. But whatever may be the exact figures, the fact is, that no richer lumber-lands exist than those of Northern New York. All that is needed for their commercial development is facility of transportation. Concerning this requisite, a writer remarks: "This access to market is, in fact, the prime want of the region. If its interior, within which the principal masses of the State lands are situated, had the means of reaching a market, the produce of the forest, in the various forms of round and square timber, sawed stuff, firewood, charcoal, and potashes, would, it is believed, pay both for the land and the clearing, — a result as desirable in the markets below as it would be beneficial to the interior."

With regard to the agricultural capabilities of this region an erroneous impression seems to prevail, the general idea being that Northern New York can never become a productive country, agriculturally speaking, that it has no natural advantages of soil and climate. This is a great mistake, for not only is the soil better adapted to grazing than many settled parts of the country, but in addition there are as many tracts of what could readily be rendered good farm-land as can be found in most regions of equal extent throughout the length and breadth of the land. Concerning certain portions of it, Professor Emmons speaks as follows: — " Contrary to the public accounts and to common opinions, I have the pleasure of stating that it is far from being the wet, cold, swampy, and barren district which it has been represented to be. The soil is generally strong and productive; the mountains are not so elevated and steep but that the soil is preserved of sufficient thickness to their tops to secure their cultivation, and most of the marshy lands may be reclaimed by ditching; by this means they will become more valuable than the uplands for producing hay. In fine, it will be found an excellent country for grazing, raising stock, and for producing butter and cheese." Again he says: " It is probable that, when the country is settled extensively, and the timber and wood removed, there will be an amelioration of climate; it will then become dryer and less frosty, and the summer warmer, and better suited to the raising of corn." Professor J. W. Benedict remarks, in his Reports of this region: "In the western section the soil in many places is deep, warm, and rich; the elevation is no greater than that of many of the most productive parts of New England, and the climate is not more rigorous. I am entirely satisfied, from repeated examination of the cattle and crops in the field and dairy in the house of the Newcomb Farm, owned by the Honorable A. McIntyre, and situated in the so-called 'Siberian region' of the Adirondacks, that it needs nothing but facilities to market, to give it distinction among those of our best agricultural districts. — Grass," he continues, "oats, potatoes, rye, buckwheat, peas, beans, carrots, turnips, onions, and cabbages, flourish in these western settlements, for aught I can see, as well as in any other part of the State. What more, then, is wanting, under good husbandry, to fill the dairies with butter and cheese, and cover the fields with sheep, cattle, and horses?"

The following agreeable picture of farm-life in St. Lawrence County is from the "Forest Arcadia":—
"There was an air of repose and comfort along the road which pleased me exceedingly. Nobody seemed to be in a hurry; the farmer who answered our questions by the roadside spoke in a tone self-possessed and calm. The fields were well cleared for half a mile on either side, and

well fenced, and the houses were generally framed, set back a little from the road, and well ordered. Beyond the clearings, and flanking them for miles, were dense groves of sugar-maples, called in this country sugar-bushes, their luxuriant plumes nodding to each other in the evening breeze as we rode by. Occasionally the tinkle of a cow-bell broke the almost perfect silence. Everything seemed wrapt in a dream of peace. — The farmer," the writer says elsewhere, " devotes himself to the keeping of cows — some farms having as many as two hundred — and the making of butter and cheese, which he can readily sell, without moving it, at the highest market-price. Instead of the severe labor in the field of preparing the ground, planting, hoeing, and reaping, his whole attention is turned to the fresh fields and pastures new that surround his modest dwelling. He milks his cows, churns his butter, smoking his pipe meanwhile with the greatest possible enjoyment."

In fact, the soil of a great part of the country seems to be considerably superior to that of New England. It is strong and rich, and although the climate is undoubtedly severe, there is no reason why the crops should not be an important element of wealth. Mr. Hammond, who visited a large portion of the region as a tourist and sportsman, states that in his wanderings he came across many spots which he trusts and believes will in the future be transformed by the hands of skilled labor into fine and fertile farms.

A large portion of the region is included in what the

agricultural writers call the Northern Highland district. Much of the soil is derived directly from the Primitive Rocks, which produce two soils, according to the variety of granite which prevails: one derived from potash felspar or ordinary coarse granite, the other lime felspar which belongs to the hypersthene rock.

Of the commerce and manufactures of Northern New York the following brief *resumé* may not be uninteresting. Potsdam, on the Racket River, has a large lumber-trade and many factories; it is also a market for the sale of the produce of the surrounding country. The lumber-trade of the Racket River, and of St. Lawrence County generally, might be made much larger and more profitable than it is at present, as might also the trade in agricultural produce. Canton, on Grass River, is a market for dairy-wealth, and as it possesses both railroad connections and water facilities, it has of course the requisites for extensive commerce and manufactures. The situation of Ogdensburg, on the east shore of the St. Lawrence, at the mouth of the Oswegatchie, — a middle ground for navigation, that of the lower waters meeting here the navigation of the lakes, and a terminus of the Northern and Rome and Ogdensburg Railroad, connecting from the east with the Prescott, and Ottawa, and Grand Trunk roads, — gives it extensive commercial advantages, and justifies the prediction that it is destined to become a great city. The Seymour House at this place is one of the best hotels in the State. Clinton County does a large business in peltries, stock-raising, dairy-produce, lumber, and the manufacture of starch, in addition to its immense iron business, and the by no means inconsiderable items of fishing and hunting. Plattsburg has a fine harbor, and extensive water facilities. Essex County contains a number of tanneries, and manufactories of sashes, blinds, tubs, pails, starch, paper, and black-lead. Ship-building is carried on to some extent, and the raising of stock and lumbering Franklin County raises agricultural and dairy produce; does a considerable business in lumber, and has over forty factories for the manufacture of starch from potatoes which, with spring grain, are largely grown here. Herkimer County does a fair business in dairy-produce, especially in the article of cheese, of which it makes three times the amount of any other county in the State. It also raises a large crop of hops, and is not deficient in general manufactures. Jefferson County comprises many limestone and slate districts which are very favorable for dairy purposes, spring grain, barley, oats, corn, rye, peas, etc.; it also contains many manufacturing depots for iron, castings, machinery, cotton and woollen fabrics, paper, leather, flour, etc., the chief of which are situated along Black River, and in Antwerp, Theresa, Philadelphia, Adams, and Ellisburgh. The building of rafts and ships is a considerable item along the St. Lawrence River. Watertown has large manufactories, and Sackett's Harbor an extensive naval station and depot. Lewis County raises dairy-produce and spring grains, and contains extensive manufactories for lumber, leather, paper, etc., along the Black, Moose, and Beaver rivers. Warren County raises dairy-produce, and manufactures leather and lumber; it also contains quarries of black marble. St. Lawrence County is the first county in the State for the raising of dairy-produce and stock, beside being rich in spring wheat, potatoes, peas, maple-sugar, lead, iron, and lumber.

CHAPTER VI.

RAILROADS; THE OPENING OF THE ADIRONDACK.

Having in the preceding chapters described in a necessarily brief way the Wilderness of Northern New York, and shown that the region abounds in valuable minerals, is rich in lumber, not deficient in agricultural wealth, and teems with manufacturing facilities, it now remains for us to indicate its chief deficiency, which is, simply, that of a railroad to develop its manifold resources.

As far as railroads are concerned, it is the veriest truism to say that the most barren and worthless district becomes comparatively fertile and valuable when once connected with the centres of trade by these great highways of civilization. How much more precious, then, the Wilderness-region will be when its wealth of mine and forest is rendered available by a railroad to New York, may easily be imagined.

Several lines of railroad are in active operation in different portions of Northern New York. The Ogdensburg, or Northern Railroad, runs from Ogdensburg on the St. Lawrence River to Rouse's Point on Lake Champlain, passing through Madrid, Potsdam, Brasher, Malone, Chateaugay, Chazy, and Moer's Point. This road is one hundred and eighteen miles in length, and is an important artery of trade. The Plattsburg and Montreal Railroad crosses the Northern Railroad at Moer's Point. The Sackett's Harbor and Ellisburgh Railroad is another line, eighteen miles in length, connecting at Pierpoint Manor with the Watertown, Rome, and Cape Vincent Railroad, which connects at Rome with the New York Central Railroad, and is ninety-seven miles in length. The Potsdam and Watertown Railroad, seventy-six and a quarter miles long, connects with Ogdensburg, passing through Canton. The railroads of Northern New York run along the Northern, North-Western, and South-Western borders, and on the south. As yet, however, no line cuts the middle of this vast region, either from east to west, or from north to south. The Adirondack Railroad, as at present completed and contemplated, fulfils to a certain extent the latter of these requisites.

The general design of the Adirondack Company is to connect the Wilderness-region, to the centre of which the part now being constructed nearly extends, with the great centres of trade. It is also to facilitate the business of the immense mining district of Northern New York, so that its large mineral resources, and more particularly its vast wealth in iron, may be developed in a manner commensurate with their unexampled magnitude.

The first important attempt to develop the wealth of the Wilderness-region was made a few years since by the organization of the "Sackett's Harbor and Saratoga Railroad Company." This project was well received both by the State and the public; special privileges were offered to the Corporation, and grants of forest-land were made to it, making an aggregate of over half a million of acres in the possession of the Company. Thorough surveys were made, resulting in the selection of a remarkably favorable line, and the work of construction was commenced with vigor. But the undertaking was unfortunately forced to yield to a financial crisis, and active operations were suspended. Various attempts were subsequently made to revive the scheme, among which was the inducing of several English capitalists to take a controlling interest in the road, but the breaking out of the Rebellion checked for the time all further enterprise. At last the affairs of the Company were wound up, a Receiver was appointed, through whom the Company's estate passed into the hands of the Adirondack Company. This result was due, in great part, to the sagacity and energy of T. C. Durant, Esq., who, perceiving the importance of the enterprise, at once applied his financial and administrative abilities to the prosecution of the work of construction.

A considerable portion of the Adirondack Railroad is already completed and in operation. Starting from Saratoga, after a ride of fifteen miles or thereabouts, we reach Jessup's Landing, or Palmer's Falls, in the township of Corinth. Here the road touches the Hudson, along whose bank it winds. Five miles farther, at Luzerne, we reach the Sacondaga River, a branch of the Hudson. Fourteen miles beyond the road strikes Schroon River, opposite and about three miles from the town of Warrensburgh. From twenty-five to twenty-eight miles farther we enter the Wilderness-region, and leave civilization behind us. Passing on our way the romantic station known as "The Glen," and the station of Johnsburg, we penetrate the heart of the forest, rushing along by streams and gorges, and amidst the most picturesque scenery for ten or twelve miles, gradually approaching the Adirondack mines and the great mineral district of Northern New York. A large portion of the road follows the original survey of the Sackett's Harbor and Saratoga Railroad. At Ord's Falls the middle section of the proposed Black Water Navigation connects with the line of road.

A great deal of local traffic must necessarily be transacted along this line. A vast amount of freight will be transported, large in bulk in proportion to intrinsic value, and therefore profitable as freight; while the passenger travel will be a very considerable item in its receipts, — an important one, indeed, in the summer or pleasure season. As the Wilderness-region becomes better known, thousands will avail themselves of its railroad facilities to visit its wild and beautiful scenery, its green and shady forests, its still and limpid lakes, its deep gorges, and its lofty mountains; and, without doubt, hotels will ere long be erected throughout this whole section of the State. The lumber will afford constant employment for the road; the agricultural produce will seek it as its avenue to market; while the immense mineral wealth of the region will tax, profitably alike to itself and the whole country, its utmost resources. There can be no doubt of the *need* of such a line as the Adirondack Railroad, nor any reasonable doubt of its ultimate success.

It will benefit the Wilderness-region and the seaboard cities through the interchange of their wealth,— the ore, the lumber, and the grain of one passing the merchandise of the other,— the forest greeting the wilderness as they hurry on their iron way, northward and southward. And it will benefit more than these; for the time is not far distant when it must benefit Canada as well, and by so doing add still further to our own riches. Middle Canada, at least, will soon seek this road on its way to our markets, and will return by it in preference to any other route. Indeed, there is no other which it can take by rail, and to suppose that it will rest content with its present deficient water communications, is absurd. There was a time when men were satisfied with stage-coaches and packets, with teams and tow-boats, but we have changed all that. The highway from Canada to New York, and from New York to Canada, is through the Adirondacks.

The coal of Pennsylvania, for instance, upon which Canada so largely depends, and which now reaches it by tardy and circuitous routes,— floating from the terminus of the Delaware and Hudson Canal up the Hudson, and through Lake Champlain,— will shortly reach its destination by this road, speeding through the wilderness to the clatter of the engine, which tosses back its long plume, and startles the solitude with its wild screams, jubilant, it would seem, at the Opening of the Adirondacks.

THE END.

www.ingramcontent.com/pod-product-compliance
Lightning Source LLC
Chambersburg PA
CBHW020158170426
43199CB00010B/1102